IMPERIUM

Jay Gao is the author of three poetry pamphlets: *TRAVESTY58* (2022); *Katabasis* (2020), a winner of a New Poets Prize; and *Wedding Beasts* (2019), shortlisted for the Saltire-Callum MacDonald Award. He is a Contributing Editor at *The White Review*. Originally from Edinburgh, Scotland, he earned his MFA at Brown University, and is currently a PhD student at Columbia University.

Imperium

Jay Gao

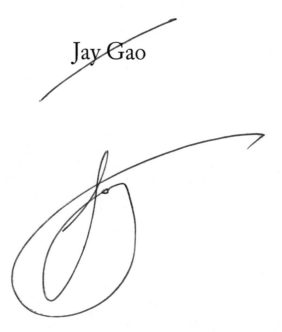

CARCANET POETRY

First published in Great Britain in 2022 by
Carcanet
Alliance House, 30 Cross Street
Manchester, M2 7AQ
www.carcanet.co.uk

A CIP catalogue record for this book is
available from the British Library.

ISBN   978 1 80017 247 0

Book design by Andrew Latimer
Printed in Great Britain by SRP Ltd, Exeter, Devon

The publisher acknowledges financial
assistance from Arts Council England.

CONTENTS

I am suspicious of heroes. How do they survive?
— Vahni (Anthony Ezekiel) Capildeo

The shipwrecked, tremulous navigator anticipates the work of the compass.
— Max Horkheimer and Theodor Adorno

I am not nostalgic. Belonging does not interest me. I had once thought that it did. Until I examined the underpinnings. One is misled when one looks at the sails and majesty of tall ships instead of their cargo.
— Dionne Brand

HERO WORSHIP

I wake to stay in bed again, decide
every minor error of mine will remain broken in its wildness.
Nights of loss now end peacefully and rarely with restless
sediment. Beyond doubt, I no longer feel alone.
Update on security incident is the subject of these siren emails;
so it seems ghosts keep trying to hack the university's global
trade routes. I dream about our sacred technicians haunting around
the anxious clock. Deep breathing. Remain
vigilant. I remind myself I am the translation machine. Excavated,
I am multiplying. In the morning, it must have snowed
even if I did not witness it.
This inert world seemed so buried with an off-white energy
yet to be exploited, and I made a gambit to get my body out of there,
a homecoming in disguise, my old return. Jupiter, Saturn,
Mercury aligned a few weeks ago without me even knowing.
Yet I could still perceive it. I think I slept right through it,
like a dress rehearsal before death.
No matter how many rooms
I gift my heroic molecules, they refuse to fall in line,
to deterritorialise. To be honest, I am excited to know what aporias
you will be planning soon, I praise our tenantless sun.
This year, I resolve to be both at home and not,
wet with words, my fingers within language
then doing without.
One childhood ambition was to project myself way into the past
like a statue.
I wanted to end by walking backwards, trace
slower circles in my back garden; in the distance,
beyond the steel mountains, I hear a train slip back into
the platform of its avant-garde station with a click, that snap of setting

a pen's cap back on. The hands of the train are lifted
straight up as if to say: Okay.
You got me. I admit it,
I yield my tempo.
Just let me surrender over
all my worlded goods to you.

IMPERIUM ABECEDARIAN

Oh! Adventurer
Oh! Boss
Oh! Coloniser
Oh! Despot
Oh! Emperor
Oh! Fascist
Oh! God
Oh! Hero
Oh! Imperator
Oh! Jailer
Oh! King
Oh! Leader
Oh! Monarch
Oh! Nazi
Oh! Overlord
Oh! Pioneer
Oh! Queen
Oh! Ruler
Oh! Sovereign
Oh! Translator
Oh! Usurper
Oh! Voyeur
Oh! Wanderer
Oh! Xénos
Oh! You
Oh! Zealot

let us start the clock

PERSONS NOT WELCOME

I left all my slippery toy soldiers on the washing machine lid
        those wet miniatures
          travel sized men I will have to scoop up in the morning

I clutched my dirty clothes to my chest like a bouquet of limbs
in last night's omen
        I was a child   lost in that hallway again
I was a newly sewn doll longing to be filled up with sand

on a branch I saw three apples   made of metal
        waiting to mutate

A bruise the size of an eye leading to
                  rust the size of my nation

HOSTIS

take care, do not know me,
deny me, do not recognise me,

shun me; for this reality
is infectious
— H.D.

Flying home, west, I hitch my pity
onto the mosquito trapped under the cling film
of this exotic dragon fruit salad. On its last long leg we shared
one vessel. Its authority to inflict human suffering unsettled me,
as I carefully ate around the heritages housing its stuck body.
I had read an article that said our kinship with them
can be most compellingly imagined through the metaphor of war.
You have killed nearly half of all the humans
who have ever lived; there is little of history left over you have not
yet touched. And so, the article explained, even expat mosquitoes
will, one day, clandestinely evolve some resistance to their poison,
artemisinin, with each new generation. Unless we modify
the fertility genes in the females; eradicate, in an entire genus,
the vector for disease. Genius
and victory. I have just watched the final scene from *In the Mood*
for Love again on this plane. I cried again.
I fled a similar unpicked itch.
Those strangler figs in Angkor Wat cosset a stonier intimacy
better left tongue-tied in the flesh. I wanted to be back on that buried
path towards enlightenment. Try again
the inauthentic itinerary for touring a mountain home for the gods.
Pavilion Indochine Hotel. Tick. Your prophylactic regimen. Tick.
Rain as warm as blood. Tick. And my hired driver for the day,
not much older than me,
chain-smoked American cigarettes, texted his boyfriend,

blared Khmer pop from his tuk-tuk camouflaged in Coca-Cola
logos. Later, left alone in a Lucky Burger, probing
the meaty dregs of a mango smoothie with a straw,
I felt like such a nobody. And how I loved that bad air. How
did it feel to have just conquered a world wonder? Plundered
it with the lens of a dirty phone assembled in Shenzhen, China.
Even the foreign ear of a guest cupped
against a wall can rob stone of all its kissing music.
The photographs of statues I kept near to my wallet like a deck
of lethal military technologies. Headless men
filled to their necks with stagnant water. Yet the mosquito and I,
we both consented to lengthen our link a little longer.
Inside our cabin ecosystem,
perfectly calibrated so that host rules reign supreme,
homesickness infects us both.
Nostalgic, I smuggle the mosquito in an old scar
behind my right ear, and listen, from its blurry world below,
for the wet choral buzzing of larva who curve
their sleep beyond muddy colonies: might they dream
of more classic things, of past lives lived out in a touched
and looted and ruined state.

In the morning the rain would not stop falling. Every tree   root
burst, collapsed inwards on their worldly rotations.   Although
I misremembered what Arendt said about divine   punishment
preventing the commission of crimes, everywhere I spied   men
in their pews still asleep, enchanted. After our coach   was
parked, fifteen minutes to furtively piss or fart outside,   stretch
our legs, steal some local sheep, before we run away. Perhaps   you
return home. You bathe your feet. Pick a fight. Grab a   stone.
Protect your wife. Hang the rest. Smash your head in for   what
you covet. The weight of my soul faded from the seat's   moquette
like the morning fog after we spiralled between the   Nationalised
Lake and its dazzling Water Treatment Plant.   Annihilative
winds formed mirages on a second shore; bold black   spots
seemed to fritz, to colonise, every inch of tempered   window
glass. I fantasised graphic empires too easily, suburban   nations
where every citizen is also the executioner, where frozen   ploughs
carve nostalgia like war horses, frauds in the fields,   frostwork
across their blades mistaking metal for a separate battle   over
income. Nothing is as real as history expunged on tour.   Nothing
changes. Whenever abroad I insist on travelling with a   second
body, a third epithet. What crimes need to be invented?   When
asked if I believed in God I told our guide: If I could choose,   I
would like to relive the epic rebirth complex. All day we   retreat
from stock exhibits too early, we hurried to flee from deep   salt
mines, the laws of house rarely yielding. Our line of   coaches
fell out of chronology like revolutionary stones forced to   skim
all day elsewhere. Starving, we returned to our hotel   chains,
made mad by the temptations from exotic fruits and plants   and
meats – You name it! We ached for fragrant fleshier   translations.

these dreams are for the pre-human

one sleep for nonsense   one giant hand slipped
into the earth
I half bury like a shield of silk   half of one inert
ritual keeping
          peace keeping
          house my fingers churned those mercantile chests
whilst gulleting in the tall grass   in the white
graves
          those suited egrets waited by the stream for their
sweetbreads

like a map each new world opens with a knife to the body
and inside I find a sweet receipt   that paper sign
the conjured phrase I did not know was so untranslatable

Hero
          what were your wanderings about

TORM SPELL

When my blue fantasy ended /   / the truth is /
        / last night /   / as you slept /   / I watched /
the belly of a pig curl upwards /
cut out on the stalling slush /
              / auspiciously /   / you and I /   / our forecast /
                            / was yet to be broadcasted /
                  / so outside all roads became /   / docile /
                        / in the mist's eternal pleasure /
        / and car engines failed like tilted hyphens in that rain /
        / I followed a splutter from behind our curtain slit /
        / glassy entrails by the blue buried shoulder /
        / I began to sense /
                                / I began to sense the recycled /
                  / auguries /
              / the reprints of hoof tracks /
the dents /   / from four rubber tyres /
              / but I had no reason /   / to wake you then /
        / the neighbour's blue pig was /
intoxicated /
in the drift /   / so all I could gift you was proof /
        / we were together /
              / frozen /
                  / fixed finally /
                            / like the violet's raw colour /
right / / at the moment /
                  / the rain shifted gears to turn into hail /
                  / those first vowels /
                  / last words /
        / you /   / said to me on instinct /
                  / before we slept /
                  / disintegrating far above our skin /

/ like tattoos waiting for their berserk ink /
/ like a bristled script waiting to be called into oblivion /
/ like an erotic code printed onto a thick blue coat /
                                        / poor pig /
                                / forced to narrate /
                        / in order to survive /
        / could it / / too / / refuse the island's atmosphere /
/ this climate's /   / frayed weather /
                / poor pig /   / poor past lives /
        / trapped in that intense bondage /
                                / of a future already /
                                / too far plotted /
/ by some advance guard /

BEESWAX

Not far from the ruins, by the latrines,   fumbling
for a foreign coin, you came to a stop, to   that
ineffable mark of slowness, stasis, earbuds   pressed
in like two bullets or errant commas. Did   you
realise then the desire to negate prefixes we   used
to celebrate, memorialise? Old lore: the wet   cut
grass near the graves, once primeval, once   curated
green with dread, now smelled vacant of   rosier
glass ghosts. Archives must be rewritten from   time
to time, yet every word which captured joy   felt
tainted here, and all our private language   risked
evasion, speech transmuting into inky steam,   so
that even the loveliest discourse became as   deep
as vintage static, like an affidavit for   pre-recorded
magic, for two monsters below two hostile   suns.

SEEING MAN (1)

On the mantlepiece a stuffed quail looms
that once relied on an infinity of forest
— Joseph Brodsky

Siwa, the Great Sand Sea. In 1885 the adventurer Luigi   Robecchi
Bricchetti called it Oasis of Jupiter Ammon. The tour guides   parked
my camel near theirs, near silver humped Ferraris which   shimmer
like spilled mercury in the heat. I would never have guessed still   life

survived inside that slippery Mountain of the Dead, caves   which
predate tourism as well as pilgrimage. In antiquity, did the   wind
pass by the openings of that human formicary, eyes with   nothing
to gaze on, no bodies to blow waywardly, no skulls waiting to   be

snapped by the feeble flash of greyscale Orientalists? In life I had   seen
enough to drink an omen wherever it springs. Later, the violet   clouds
opened above a silver lake; and the martyred sunset burst   outwards,
out of its sky-skin, like flesh from an overly ripe date. Yesterday   you

told me about the news of a suicide bomber in a market in   Sinai.
Paradoxically, what's the difference when someone kills via   drone
button versus the hero who kills with their own body, his   quest
leaving no citations. Mbembe says: *To kill, [the suicide bomber]   has*

to come as close as possible to the body of the enemy. To detonate the   bomb
necessitates resolving the question of distance. In the end little   reflects
the glint of war and all it distantly ruins. I spied a gang of   golden
daffodils plotting by the polluted pools of the Oracle. Were   they

once German soldiers seeking shade, skinny dipping their   epic
bodies in those waters? I met our weekend cabal at our   luxury
hotel. Metropolitan citizens to include one heiress of a   Chinese
African-media mogul; one descendent of Robin Maugham ('...all

the habits of today come from what happened in the past... '); two
Ivy-league digital nomads, newly graduated, upper-middle   class
children of immigrants; three sun-burnt but tenured   academics
cloddishly trading abstracts on dead ethnologists; some   off-duty

foreign aid workers on R&R; and a gay military officer   whose
uniform bears a rainbow flag stitched below a flag of his   authoritarian
nation. He spends his time fantasising about a haven slash   base
here, where '...*such agreements continued, but in great secrecy,   and*

without the actual writing, until the end of World War II... '   Then,
at a second camp, kept far enough from ours, a conference   of
reconciliation groups, advocates for transitional justice,   reparations,
truth commissioners for survivors of genocide and ethnic   cleansing –

they too have earned a little time off, some cool leisure after   their
veiny tribunals. I stared at us; I stared at our corpse-lives. Then   I
began to picture the pain of others, how the ground we rested   on,
loved on, paid for, was so pristinely haunted and occupied by   those

eidolons adrift from time. The Long Range Desert Group,   hungry
to fight the Empire of Japan, or the Afrika Korps, or the   136th
Armoured Division Giovani Fascisti – all these actors   centre-stage
in a theatre of sand, in someone else's souvenirs. At dinner we   knelt

beneath an asylum of fake palm trees like understudies vying   for
history's shade. A metal net trapped the light above the foliage,   lost
empires glinted on its canopy as red dust hummed on winding   sheets.
Welcome! our noble five star-rated host, evening Oracle,   proclaims.

Young men then carry out, so we are told, an authentic dish of   ram's
head buried in hearts of palm. Is it still tradition to tip here?   *Stay*
forever! Eat until you explode, a standard host joke. Like a globe   whirls
after it is spun he then goes around our tent one by one to prove   he

can small talk in as many languages as there are time zones;   later,
he will twist his tongue, rip us off, earn commission for every   mass-
produced specialty copper coffee pot we adore to drink out of   and,
as if bewitched, cannot resist purchasing. He declares that I must   be

Japanese. I choose not to correct him. To push him for a   further
discount I will tell any minor lie: *Just a memento for a friend I   love.*
No, not a girl. Two friends. Twin beds. To you, the only other   British
national, he recites a standard line from Wikipedia: *The first   European*

to visit Siwa since Roman times was the English traveller William   George
Browne, who came in 1792, to see our ancient temple, who was   murdered
in 1813 on his attempt to travel to Tehran. Was I paranoid to read   our
lucent omen in that future he professed as a chance invocation,   a

divination to be ashamed of every night, every year, until when,   until
this water runs dry. Unlike ordinary goods, did I believe words   accrue
power to solidify their custom futures the more they are   declared?
I recalled a sentence from Henry James I copied down on the   plane:

If you wish to continue the
adventure, turn to page 74.

If you wish to try a different
myth, turn to the next page.

EULOGY FOR ELPENOR

I longed to terraform a hydraulic   empire,
silent nation with state of the art   oceans,
waterscapes, both natural and   speculative
catastrophes. Wet ports with no decks   to
smuggle your vesselled cargo or   possessions
overseas, your ancient customs. How   can
I cruise a non-native body in the body   of
a ship? In the margins of a galley: an   epic's
wreck. My borderless mission was   always
to rest, to slow time down a little,   descend
a little, wait a little differently, mourn   a
little more, to sink that sun, lose this   war,
return to our bloated coast a little,   become
a little too modern; so that I could   learn
to flow, to love, to curse, to fill out   these
splendid censuses, whisper irrigated   verse
to extinct birds and other classical   denizens,
to circle back and bury any loosened   foot-
notes in the sand with the most tender   of
contracts marked onto fraternity   paddles.
In a hundred years I might return to   find
your eyes chewed through by new   regimes
of invading worker ants dreaming of   one
precarious word to free them from   their
homely fealties. I celebrated your tan,   your
smile, your green willingness to wage   hot
war. So when my late tribute came out   as
wordless as the long indelible line   refusing
erasure, each countersentence formed   scars
swimming across the sea's skin, I admit   our
midnight territories did seem as   everlasting

as traces of the mythic invisible ink we   tried
to ship, as dim as the soft inside curve   from
a blue shield shared, broken, bent way past   its
form, disoriented, still raised high after   we

NOSTALGIA

Although advised that ghost stories were an   acceptable
topic of conversation, I was still surprised to   discover
small-talk sucks up all the time in the afterlife.   After
my death, my first true appraisal is to be forced to   host
a nation-warming party. I have to invite all those   bullying
argonauts from my childhood who now arrive,   matured,
with the full gamut of their remorse. First, I ushered   them
into the living room, then left to fetch a platter of   finger
foods, the egg from the last ever bird on the planet I,   a
few hours earlier, hastily pureed into a delicious   aioli
without guilt. Upon my return I found those lads   at
rest, collected fondly together, like a pile of pink   petals
trembling from an old gifted lotus root left to me   with
zero instructions of care. What am I to do with you,   I
asked myself, staring down at the shed skin of my   ripe
guests. I pushed their legion presents to one side,   every
bottle of wine sloshed as if it contained a set of   gears,
a trapped clock waiting to be let out, to turn into a   ship.
Later, when the lads are partying on the roof, when   I
am tasked to clean up their inevitable carnage,   their
broken bottle-necks, their crisp packets, their   loosened
morale, I forget the most vital host rule – that *the   living
are obliged to prepare a banquet for the past*; even after all   my
mortal practice, time preparing for the life that comes   after,
I was never taught how to invite the dead back onto the   table,
how to break bread with ghosts. No guidebook   instructions
for signalling a civil time for my strangers to exit   tonight.

BODY SONNET

I.

Behind us

I had a dream you returned to me in the borderlands

II.

There is no doubt remaining in our day

that imperial history has to be repeated every night,

III.

Re-open time like the cloche on our

    earbuds pressing themselves in

        dream-brought.

      There is the nonviolence of one into stone into

IV.

did the breath of those

inert evenings feel celestial even before a thing of joy

hospital windows from the last night ever.

I wanted to end it by any natural means; one last plea for what is

subjected.

v.

what could I do or travel to in order

    to order his body into a space not filled in with tradition

        a ghost ship glides in like the ending.

           I was in an enormous beyond;

                I believed in the grey water

                    in a diver,

                        a sedated rubber tyre.

VI.

Abecedarian work

I fantasise what I could do

sleep, wake, herd his opinions on religion

and things

and

VII.

bewilder if you can.

Like it if you could almost presage his language.

I didn't know you would be stateless.

If I did

I would have ceased from

VIII.

these nations

found he himself had changed history.

   he was a beggar back in the real world

      he, who never conquered what

IX.

Oh!

Zealot There is nothing free of bass still asleep,

he found he had transformed into

X.

Hero,

what were you at the time;

      setting fire to the larger picture;

      setting fire to the protest on the surface;

      settling   down

XI.

one sleep slipped into the centre

of the air, through his Chinese doors, like a bouquet

                              banquet

XII.

Last night over our valley a version of me never became domesticated.

I fled to flee from another sweet trap,

an oil

XIII.

I wonder if you covet. The weight of my soul

faded from a foreign guest, never preventing the epic

XIV.

My heart

The sand,

the blood

in

the water?

Should be

an illusion

NOBODY

Yes, it begins with the skin
— Nicole Brossard

In the skin, through the skin, the world and the body touch, defining their common border.
— Michel Serres

You were seeking an immaculate theory to save you from the hotel bar. A universal sign, a manifestation of your future existence in the weave of the doily underneath your bowl of stale peanuts. Or perhaps a monologue sprung from the oceanic currents divined in the mouldy mint compass on your watery julep. At a distance, can strange hosts sense urgency in the mind better than hostility broadcasted out on the limbs? Who else in this hotel was longing for an elemental connection? Has any chance hospitality ever been paid back in full by a short script, a little betrayal, or some other ugly sentence?

◇

It was not difficult to decipher the notifications on your screen; in fact, you could almost presage the language, word for word, as if you had acted out this masked character role many times in a past life or two, alongside their forgettable and ambiguous endings. Each new push made your phone pulse with a glow that should belong to a rare but irradiated anemone, like a lush distant flare on a faraway island nobody was ever going to scry nor discover, for at least a few more hundred years.

◇

Be proud, champion! You tamed the lion. Valiant paladin. You were never afraid. Mostly just bored. This island is full of noises and quests that sweeten the air. The buffet table mewls underneath steel platters of aphrodisiac foods shipped from distant lands. Light jazz stumbles in from the reception like released, recently anaesthetised, hostages. As if you were a beast reintroduced, you never noticed the state-of-the-art mosquitoes, engineered to carry nothing, until after you were bitten; an inoculating spectacle, a red archipelago of bumps rising irritant, itching to be bathed in seawater. They can sense sugar in your sweat, in your sweet blood; your mother used to warn about those twisted physicians, predictors of lineal, unavoidable, diabetes.

◇

Last night you heard a mosquito curse close then far then close again to your ear nearest to the pillow, like a swelling grand piano being tuned in an adjacent suite. All day you scratched at the humming wound, that weal in the fossa of your ear, not realising you were even doing it, where a small gem of sap had grown like a crystal waiting to be mined. So the tempo of air felt charged forever, and all speech was made strange by your immune responses. You wish you were back in your hotel bed, listening to the scandal of a rainstorm loop through your headphones, whilst it rained outside too, spectral choruses inside the white noise machine, primal archetypes inside the blacklight, sometimes waking you up, sometimes making you sleep or squirm again, sometimes making you dream you were crying, sometimes making you dream you were raining. You think you see her, there in the clouds' music, but the distant figure is never your mother, she is only the pale dust of lightning as it splits a ship in two.

◇

Receiving messages from him was like hinging your body towards the past tense. *Nearly there. In taxi now. What are you wearing?* Upon looking up, the Translator opposite you has vanished, slipped out like a shibboleth. No trace left but her cautious crumpled tissue holding a discrete lipstick stain and, perhaps, the weak scent of a lavender flowerhead hastily rubbed in earnest as it mingled with the oppressive humidity of this nation, unravelling behind her ear, against her shoulder-blades, across each wrist. Her book's title stayed with you long after she packed it away. *Time is the Thing a Body Moves Through.* You wanted to follow the direction of that discipline; you wanted to be the subject of that book, to go with its story, her lead, her stage exit. Look, there is the tip she need not have left. You ordered a cultural fusion cocktail you thought she might have enjoyed. You were acutely aware of a kind of celestial time passing through every atom of you that evening as if you were caught up in a great wave, so that the lavish past folded up to press against your present, as if you were just a ghost from the underworld counting down the seconds until your own molecular dissolution.

◇

Time's measure kept dividing in half before you, beyond you, first splitting before segmenting, soothing before punishing, like the peach slice floating on your rum's rubbery soup; cut half and half further until its sweetness is overcome by the diffuse Sichuan peppercorns in the background of your throat, all that distance travelled through the air nulled in just one swallow: a totalising, lip-numbing, destruction of the self condemned to meaning.

◇

How dare these other guests concede you zero moments, so little action? Too preoccupied with their own intimate dramas, you think. They seemed to be privately working against you in every possible way. You thought their facial expressions resembled those of settled soldiers or expatriate spies, but how would you ever know who is real, who was merely on expedition. Everyone wore a disguise, pretending to be a tourist. Round mouths, all praising and bringing, into this time period, a warning from a different reincarnation. He never chose to meet at the most expensive bar in this hotel; that would be the French restaurant, *Le Royal*, well admired across the world for its ability to overlook the famous ruins from an infinity pool a few floors up. Its sign *Kindly, No Locals Allowed*, sometimes brought out on those hot days when, everywhere and elsewhere, across the margins of the city, elderly bodies give out one last exhale on their beds, on the curb, on the train, at work, their eyes rolling up like how a body, shaped into a cannonball, might slowly rise in the pool. After the initial spray of bubbles, after the water settles again, your attention lingers for a second on the view through the smog before it evaporates towards eternity.

◇

Who adorned this bar in all its camp colonial fodder? Dark wood varnished in some synthetic chemical, a sinewy discharge pulsing from each panel. An invisible wound will never heal. A memory of a weapon, a hand, a pen, once thrust inside an opening. A body holding back its imperial breath. The fake books on the shelves could never be cut open to record the price of commodities or ancient verb-tables. You could break off those lamps which drooped like dim melted daffodils. You could bring those twigs to your ear, politely nod along to their galvanic complaints, remind them you are not the staff here. *Then what are you?* Motorised fans moved as languidly as history, pushing nothing around in their perpetually slow revolution setting, a lazy threat of decapitation. Behind the table of sweating artichokes, oysters, figs orbited by flies, resting watermelon slices weeping like meat, seven grandfather clocks prognosticate, from the seven most vital cities on the planet, that there will always be sunlight beating down ceaselessly onto the pale skin of one timezone. Even the repeating wallpaper print, the same two continents from some cliché voyage of discovery, is mapped out indefinitely; its pattern threatened to trap you in its endlessness if not for that visible wall seam bisecting those islands, unevenly paired, pushed together, two irregular and jagged borders, one contact zone.

◇

So you tell yourself to relax, to believe in the lore, in the objectives of this quest. There will always be a rupture or incision the hero can hide in, new symbols you cannot tell apart, one familiar eye in the paper walls of the cave calling out your fake name on an application that traffics in its globalisation. You yawn, you order another drink, you repeat your mantra that *the local is the only universal, upon that all art builds*, you decide tomorrow you will monetise that, you cross your legs, angling them towards the sum of the infinite.

◇

The nights abroad should not progress sequentially but are opportunities for subversion, far away from your homely duties. You exploit those right and critical moments. An arrow fired with enough force to penetrate a character. A shuttle passing through the threads of a loom. The instant of an aperture. A punctum hovers in the air, waiting to be looted. The precise work of force driven through in order for your dreams and passions to become reality. *Exercised to the limit, it turns man into a thing in the most literal sense: it makes a corpse out of him. Somebody was here, and the next minute there is nobody here at all; this is a spectacle.* You are not sure you agree with this citation. Could you incorporate it back through your body? What if your story depended on it? What if the fate of an entire civilisation was at risk?

◇

Right when you begin to wonder if his taxi was involved in some horrific collision, there he appears, a survivor of your tamest revenge fantasies. Only a few metres away now. Somewhere in that building. Anonymous. But not really like a bird at all. He was on his way up. No, not like one bird in any one way. *I'm here.* He was getting nearer, warmer. All the blood pumping through the bodies in the bar felt as hot as molten lead coming to a vital boil. It was that time of night when everyone starts to transform into their own island's automaton. *You are so hot. I am so hot for you.* He always writes the same message as if stuck inside a time-loop taking on the form of a monsoon. He wants to bind you here forever. If every word enunciated is magic, does silence risk the death of every exotic beast, every island host? Like too many books lent out to too many friends, these are all fast becoming your responsibilities. You circle the length of the menu three times with your eyes. Still, you think, he can speak and write how he desires; he lets you buy the most expensive drinks. But you hate that you will have to beg him to pay that bill, to sign his name, swipe his platinum Amex card. You begin to understand that it's not so odd every drink here is nicknamed *The Colonel* or *The Admiral* or *The General* or *The Hero*.

◇

Years ago, his first message was: *I want to save you from this place*. And during which holiday did he buy you a Hermes scarf decorated with a scene of nude men fighting from *The Iliad*. You feigned not knowing how to pronounce ekphrasis. You feigned not knowing Greek. You feigned that the tradition was too impersonal, too far removed from your plural realities. Yet, you must admit, occasionally, you did masturbate to that shame, to replicating an exotic unknowability in your performances, your margins as wide as the edges of a tempest, that great force of distance made to be closer. You never wanted to give him the privilege of knowing your education, your life story, your name. You never wanted to be a minor trickster deity. Because, all along, you knew the hero in the world must always return home, no matter the cost; you won't even realise you are homed until it is right in front of you, but by then it will already be far too late.

◇

Later that night, over the door of the room he had booked, the number eight looked like they were the plucked eyes from a hallway bust of a magistrate's head made to lie down on a pillow sideways. You noticed how every turn of these labyrinthine corridors looked identical. You hoped this was a maze that could never be solved. If solved, if translated, the only option would be to throw yourself off a cliff like a last monster, a final boss.

◇

Was it too late to be a comparatist? Here are two memories to thread an escape from: once, on a school trip in the heart of Europe, you felt your own face enveloped in the glow of a Greek statue staring down. You were at an exhibition on how avant-garde civilisations rise before collapsing. The model of the marbled male, whose sculptor you cannot remember, bathed you in his wordless geometries; and compare that with your dismay that no expression from any of the oxidised soldiers in the Mausoleum of the First Qin Emperor ever provoked a similar resonance. Never made your skin hot with a potential to wake up stone or terracotta, never making you risk crossing a boundary that leans itself towards transformation. In real life, their bodies seemed too minor and anonymous, buried inside a vast pit, the viewing platform built above them. And the nearby recreated statue of an archer, with its original paint reapplied, seemed so ugly that you preferred his skin to be leached of colour, to have been damaged in the process of his bruised unearthing.

◇

You wanted to text him, *if I could kill you I would then have to make another exactly like you.* Thinking back, you already had the question then you ask yourself now. Why are you here? Why are you here looking at me?

◇

All throughout the night you worried about the growing distance between your soul and that Translator you never spoke to at the bar. That temporality first seemed to increase in polite increments, but soon accelerated like a fighter jet gaining speed, as it crosses a threshold of no return. How hard can it be to track down a ghost? You let her go. You must close your eyes and breathe. Lie back and think of antiquity. Half of the time of her brief, non-existent, connection lasted in your mind as you, your eyes rolled up towards the ceiling, glazed over with the clairvoyant morning fog over a sea; the jagged white swirl of the ceiling design, the same in all the rooms you have ever lived in, reminded you of the whirlpool Charybdis, and her unquenchable frothy thirst, who even heroes will choose to avoid when given the choice, only one length of an arrow away from her sister. Would you rather act the conscious monster of the strait, or embody the violent flow of tides, unthinking citizen?

◇

Your black hair swirled around in the shower, your voice coming and going, as you tried to tiptoe through an anti-personnel conversation coming in from the bedroom you could not hear. You think the precarity of your life depended on the flawlessness of your twinkling responses. But how can you answer a question you do not hear? *Far, far from you world history unfolds, the world history of your soul.* You open your mouth to speak but there's only the glut babble of water urgently becoming scalding. Your sense of self goes under; time dilates inside you, the steam makes you vibrate with a foreign impermanence, until you already start to forget first the face of the Translator at the bar in the water, then your own name in the morning.

◇

You record her book's title down on your phone incorrectly: *The Body is a Thing Time Moves Through*. Some people get off on taking photographs of strangers without them knowing; you, instead, manoeuvre that camera lens inside your head to flip it back onto yourself. Zooming out you clearly see your two legs dangling from the stool, still a little too tense, a little too strict. You indulge in what it might symbolise if they were to hang down from the wooden beams of the bar's tropical fetish instead. Imagine if, all evening, you had no other plans than to have your limbs be captured, and supported high up there by two tender hooks. Imagine being that mauled body they find in a field from a film you watched yesterday by a Thai director; there were always two versions to that story, one in which you could be hung up on a tree, waiting to be silently transported when morning arrives.

◇

Within the architecture of an alternative ending the happy hour would never end, and you had all the queer time in the nation to drink your fill, to kill the time of heroes, to conduct an autopsy on all the covert anatomies underpinning the set you are so keen to disturb and agitate, to sneak out in the morning like a wake from a ship, to go outside where the monsoon shower was as warm and pulsing as blood, to unwind and drown in its droplets that fell heavy on your skin; the rain was wordless, sentient, each able to carry a mutilated world, but each, no matter what, each, no matter your preferences, your influences, longing to return to a greater body yet to be judged as the most irresistible in the suspicious minds of the others.

◇

Once this poem ends, so will the rain.

BODY SONNET

I.

                    I clutched the soil barely approving.

Slipped into stone right away.

Remember lichen glowed like a stressed syllable on the last ginkgo

branch   as he landed.

II.

what fire to displayer

      our city was like a tonne,

         a non-nation,

abandoned. You feign me

      curtains craving

         which english

III.

Witness steps from another satin body,

There, near my voice, haunted hunted hung

from every word took to fire like a monstruth

IV.

let us and us and us and us another,

    let one fully desire their customs;

V.

We arrived.

Translating winds of lines:

You vein me kindly. Glass flitters

VI.

you were my guest

What goes without saying why

wetend fledturn frozenfeel every sandreed

you knocked over

VII.

Imperial breath of those frozen viaducts overturned to overtake us.

VIII.

                              these the buds left

above wished through missing landscaping.

Witnessing myself as unplaced heat here

      or there or

IX.

he white time zones lazuli of the paused city

X.

No full story here

     a nearby thumb deep in argument processes travel like a

     kiss beyond the blinking;

XI.

what hospitality

what same towns

Home

              this yet to me, give me back my rest

XII.

I received

this calling nation of branchest or beat lake. the hail detonated silently

nothed

the fish

You have to understand

The end of the muse slipped into the day not like viral cells.

XIII.

He was on the isthmus and I was gloriously late to meet him.

Ciphers of blood shooting back,

Our relation is the conjured phrase I could not speak

      Please

        World

           Let me go

XIV.

No full stop

I had a question mark of an accent; as unplaced between grief and away,

    as

unplaced myself

If only to lift the lid

    those travel documents never pass far enough

SEEING MAN (II)

I think the sirens in The Odyssey *sang* The Odyssey, *for there is nothing more seductive, more terrible, than the story of our own life, the one we do not want to hear and will do anything to listen to.*
— Mary Ruefle

You have the imagination of disaster and see life indeed as ferocious and sinister. That night, postcolonial revenge via violent   gastroenteritis.
Luckily my new phone model functions as a potent searchlight;   but
if one grain of sand gets into its charging port, you warned, it's   all

over for this trip, our images, our queer memories. So I went back   to
bed and, as if carrying on the heaving duties from our host, I   invited
strangers and their stranger dreams inside. I witnessed a   songbird
massacre I must have once read about, a slaughter gauntlet in the   air

where branch knots warbled like restless calluses, and every   meshed
acacia trapped a tail or quaver chest, now welded onto the hot   lime
anointed bark from earlier. All the fowls on fire in this Old   World.
Supposedly, *Alexander the Great brought his conquest here by   following*

birds across the sand. Did feathers drift like ash on the wind   then?
Electronic mating trills, wire-rooted, looped out of stereos disguised   as
wood, blurting odes to lure another flock. Crossing birds came to   rest
just to die in this oasis. Silent skies emptied as our manic   poaching

fingers rubbed their bijou hearts like cocked bayonets.   Every word
was as light as eating a wing. Human. Divine. Carrion. My   academic
conscience kept saying *I would rather suffer evil the natural way,* but   I
did it anyway. After the act was done the scent of plum trees,   boiled

to make a gummy snare, wafted all across the night like a bag of   wind.
I made one cairn whistle with the spat out bones of crushed   thrushes,
skulls blown in by the kiss of metal, impotent throats from   quails,
orioles, chaffinches – but I could not erase the feeling that these   were

also human bones. In my story I refused to stare into the eyes of   the
Amazigh child who watched us eat our parts only to offer a   bitter
epilogue: Better birds fallen and not bombs in the end. Yet I   awoke
feeling like I was not so far from that quiet cenotaph I built but   only

a few seconds or centuries ago to worship at. What were the   lines
etched on its stele which I brought back on my tongue, the old   verse
I re-translated under our netted tents, wondering which life   was
real, whose dream I dreamt: *I arise and unbuild it again.* As   dawn

arrives at the oasis we have nothing left to sacrifice or get wet   but
empty pages in our passports; the raw light turned our bodies   into
transparent glass, weeping, impenetrable. I asked our Oracle if I   could
buy a skin's second gambit, a holograph to grow, to make mine, if   I

tried and really desired two. Every day traded the same. Sand   seemed
to alter so little. In this life I know my organs float on bodies of   water
consistently, regardless of their owner; I have travelled enough   times
to know that no act can stay dry, pure, without implication,   forever.

I know you must have sensed queerly last night too because in   the
morning you said nothing, only sketching anarchic tidewaters   where
a bullet of ice mutates into a silver eel before stabilising on a   wedding
ring. Ahistorical interference in the natural ebb, in what is deemed   as

commonplace. There were many blue bodies on the oasis foam   that
day, many variations of organising glass. In the end the great pool   was
so shallow we sat in it like imperial debris plucked from   underwater
archives, salt-rusted statues reanimated just to play pretend at   ancient

customs. On wide ceremonious deckchairs as white as lotuses   we
complained about the price of iced drinks, vector-borne   diseases,
faraway wars now no longer so faraway, and the drought which   might
not end by natural means. Last night, rumours that a   mythological

beast invaded or escaped the gardens of this bio-reserve. Were   we
fast asleep, too busy in our domestication to capture changing   river
tracks, to document those rituals all around us, those symbols   of
rising seas, punctuated chronicles, a sun swelling in a song to   solicit

the new tourist season. On the last day before we flew home I   slipped
our Oracle an extra note in search of a terminal forecast. His   answer
was as clear as a pack of tepid bottled water. I was to ask you next   time
we were alone and true: *Do you really think we can live on like   this?*

*If you decide to continue the
adventure, turn to page 20.*

*If you wish to try a different
ending, turn to page 87.*

AGENT ORANGE

Not that I want to be a god or a hero
Just to change into a tree, grow for ages, not hurt anyone
— Czesław Miłosz

Two mandarins she wrapped in pink tissue for the temple shrine
have not decayed one bit, in half a year, since she last
left them kneeling on their imitation gold saucer.
She wished for them to mutate into twins:
one ordinary girl, one ordinary boy,
one waxy orb a little larger, leaning on its sibling, green rinds
scented with a firmness to persist forever,
smooth chemicals circulating in their peels,
altering the curling of sandalwood smoke from her joss stick,
raised up like a laurel branch.
So she directs the same prayer to her eldest son who, an ocean away,
is now the same age Arthur Galston was
when, as a green graduate student in Illinois,
he used acid to coax flower buds and fruit out of baby soybeans
so they would mature faster than nature
willed it. Before he later studied how peas might squirm or shrug
indifferently to various angles of light brought close
then far, he dreamt the research in his twenties
could heal a hungry world; but the more he fed
his specimens, the more his crops undressed themselves,
blooming into their unravelling lack, losing colour,
losing structure, until
every leaf fell from every body, and
every leaf dissolved into nothing, and
every body became a fine spray from a helicopter one might mistake
for the morning mist on the mangroves.
In that unseen contract between plant cell and foreign
agent, Arthur studied many lifecycles sped up to their unnatural

limits, unable to foresee how fast
the future might travel in all directions, with its relentless
momentum,
whenever an endpoint is forced too early. At the shrine she
hears a jingle and, for one instant,
everything is paused, sacred, and slow.
She considers taking down her ancestral fairy lights
but the LED bulbs still command respect as they pulse through
rainbow spectrums on time delayed currents,
on then off then on again, communicating to each other covertly
like ungerminated seeds,
like a corpse blinking one eye open then the other,
like a code flashed from a shard of armour in the heart of a cave.
In front of the plastic Buddha replica, two electric candles
flicker with a wildness like cogongrass,
demanding new batteries; she hovers her hand between them
like the false memory of a rain cloud; and perhaps she
senses the latency of heat recollect before refracting,
suspend before strengthening, past the variegations of her skin,
the same way a colourless liquid might become more saturated,
not less, as it moves from one body to another body –
you know –
it's like when Celan writes *the image spawns
a child with it, half image and half veil,*
like when a veil coddles the surface tension of a sea
before ripping it apart, the split
chest of a wooden ship
that used to be a child.

HOSTEL

Camouflaged in the hostel's fire alarm I retreated to my   skeleton
bunk. As I sank into its exposed foam, my worldly   exhaustion
squeezing out lifeless black ants from every sweat pore,   like
an interrupted army on a skin of clay, so I looked around   me,
witnessing those archetypes from the dorm's alien   occupants
littered on their sheets like loosened haloes; and, as if I   were
being crowded out by invisible ghosts, I heard the buzz of   bass
playing from one headphone bud left above me, and as the   drunk
gap year students danced on the hostel roof, I found it   unnerving
to catalogue all their trinkets of metamorphosis, a map, a   dictionary,
a jockstrap, a silk scarf, a ticket stub, their designer cases   bursting
open like imported organs all over the linoleum, so near to   me,
vast layers of red fabric scattered like the softest ore,   travelling
ceremonials out of reach on their beds. I think I had   disturbed
the room with my mortal presence there, the navy sheet of   the
stained bedding twitched over my knees like a borrowed   skin;
I knew that as I sat in their beds I risked soon being   walked
upon, that right away I would be unmasked as an invader,   and
become as unwanted as a species infamous for its   parasitism.

some say epochs later the Translator moved into the sublet sleeping so
    close to his asylum of hot earth
some say the Translator noticed a surplus of abandoned beds but zero
    doors zero windows
some say the runoff air from the factory vents burnt away the protective
    linings on their organs
some say they were one unspeakable contract away from becoming
    compacted into a precious fossil
some say like a napkin is stained through with fresh white wine the
    Translator folded up the corners of their skins within those
    molten micro-histories
some say to be rescued from the hungry angels in the sacked cities
some say to be rescued from the sacred technicians in the archives
some say to be carried down in his cave in the dark
some say to reciprocate his extension of hospitality and glorious
    resourcefulness
some say to be occupied indefinitely
some say to survive

                    is the most beautiful thing

some say yesterday a draught that must have once been a person
    caused the weft of their mosquito nets to blow apart, to break
    down, to disassemble themselves
some say it was as if a woman in white unravelled as she fled
some say she bolted towards a distant rockfall in a story involving
    trapped minors
some say she stacked up those stones from the inside like poison pills
some say to harbour doubt about how poor he proclaimed he was
some say to harbour suspicion about what he used to do in a past life
some say to harbour misgivings when he said he was a beggar back in the

real world
some say *the past is never dead. It's not even past*
some say to cook those priceless bison etchings carved onto the cave
      walls
some say to make sense of that wriggling punctuation mark he carried
      across his shoulders one day
some say you have to use the metaphor that it was as small as a child
      kicking and pleading
some say for its mother   But I say

      it is how we divide that head of the last white doe
            calling out to be rationed
                     for eternity
                           in this loveliest nation of two.

HOSTILE

Escaping to the shared shower blocks so early   I
assumed nobody would catch me undress. I   found
the Translator's blue towel on the rails, the   door
unlocked, water sounds not falling quite far   enough;
sewn into the centre of the air, through the tea   stained
curtain, I could make out his body's border   appear
like a ghost in my vision of a world carved out   from
lapis lazuli, and would he have believed me if I   told
him I was not the one stalking him, not the   one
hunting him, but that I was there to save his   life,
being led into his sweet trap. I could not see   clearly,
not really; I left my glasses on my bunk so I   could
only see a few steps in front at a time, as if I   were
walking through imperial mist or steam or   one
polluted morning where every near thing   seemed
one lost archipelago away, as unplaceable as   my
accent, as unmoored as the strange passing   seasons.

WHERE THERE IS BREAD THERE IS MY COUNTRY

I lost my bearings in endless future routes
when the hysterical fugue lifted   our hometowns swallowed
their fixed borders like pills   twenty-first century remedies
made a resort of those virtual great lakes

I pricked my lips tactically on the last artificial rose frozen by the banks
I returned to rest in the lantern husks of ships and coaches
I found life in the smouldering train carriages
and spotted red fox wisps
            sneering by the overturned   first class dining carts

nostalgic serow herds slow and sonorous circled outside the labyrinth

so bury me off the path   and as testimony let our bulbous sun
irradiate the final duet of green herons   jousting overhead
I was unaware of those evicted rooms which multiplied within me
            without regulation

where's the glory inevitably killing the dead twice over

Home
                if I could be granted a homecoming that would cure me

IMPERIUM

Re-open the question of power
— Hortense Spillers

How do you know this man,
>
Are you his next of kin,
>
How would you define your relationship,
>
Can you be a little more precise,
>
Where were you at the time,
>
And can you prove it,
>
What was his emotional state when you last saw him,
>
Had there been an incident,
>
An accident,
>
One that led to him going missing,
>
Do you often fight,
>
Do you drink often,
>
Has he ever self harmed,
>
Has he ever expressed suicidal tendencies,
>

Has this ever happened before,

>

Would you consider him vulnerable,

>

Would you consider him risky,

>

A risk to others perhaps,

>

Would you tell us any concerns we should be aware of,

>

Would you,

>

Would you really,

>

How would you describe him,

>

What kind of a person is he,

>

What was he like when you last saw him,

>

What was he wearing,

>

Do you recall,

>

How can you be so certain,

>

Do you have a recent photo,

>

One we could use,

>

One we could keep,

>

Do you have anything of his,

>

A toothbrush,

>

Maybe a shirt he wore,

>

A lock of hair,

>

A licked stamp,

>

A shredded postcard,

>

A shared razor,

>

His diary,

>

His pieces of a broken compass,

>

An inventory of all the islands he has visited,

>

An inventory of all the objects he has touched,

>

An inventory of all the bodies he has kissed,

>

An inventory of all the books he has read,

>

Do you know why we are asking for this,

>

Do you understand,

>

Why we think his life may be extinct,

>

Do you,

<

REST AND RECUPERATION

Our treaty to let off time, to give it up, spend a month
or two in his inherited villa.
I pressed my lips to his family's Chinese tiles and sensed
my authority pass; a year yawns and all the spider plants have flushed
limp before dying. Although never followed
into the blue cliffs, we kept missing our turn, the leap,
so had to double-back, utter every direction twice.
These early hours were ripe for stealing galvanised
bodies from history. Nobody ever caught the interlopers.
Through the benthic rain I misheard a voice that sounded like his
reciting my last name in a dream. In reality,
every wind rose swelled from the toxic water and minerals
in the pipes. He told me a story. He once tried to end his life here;
he asked if he could show me.
I looked back in time and saw him naked by the Judas tree,
violently pulling out lineal weeds and roots and tears,
blotting armies of cardinal flowers closing up, shrinking
down, ending their chemical ballet.
In that precarious realm we shared, I undressed his cold
wet self as I might pluck the invasive species off this private property.
I imagined washing off a year of conflict proximity.
Like Andromache I turn the stiff taps one way and wait
a century before turning them off again,
realising nobody's home but us.
My eyes fell on the same wound in the horizon of a timeline,
an island translated by its own tainted independence,
an island where one flag blushes its colonised tricolour,
and one viper writhes in the monochromatic wind
or bed linen. Go back to sleep, I asked of him.
His car alarm detonated not far enough from the hypogeum.
Ringing out, the gulls guarded their tourist tombs with Rilke's

invocation: *There were many quiet, rigid rules for death.* And I knew
he had chosen to play pretend, breathe through each
for both of us as we slept back to back,
touching like rare metals.
Outside even the local town, lacking glamour, began to slide
into its own near catastrophes. For example, the whitewashed pumice
smoothed out from the cloying acid rain
like a once crumpled piece of paper. One endangered moth alighted
silently, ready for its annihilation. And two
spotted lizards scurried across our walls without trial,
vatic, pale, unfair like weighted dice
cast against a future song.

ACKNOWLEDGEMENTS

Alongside all cited epigraphs and quotations, some unattributed lines in *Imperium* borrow from, in order of appearance, Walter Benjamin, John Dewey, Simone Weil, Anne Carson, Franz Kafka, Henry David Thoreau, Percy Bysshe Shelley, William Faulkner, and Sophocles. The Body Sonnets were drafted via a Travesty Generator, originally written by Hugh Kenner and Joseph O'Rourke (1984); I first came across this algorithmic poetry scrambling tool in Lillian-Yvonne Bertram's *Travesty Generator* (Noemi Press: 2019).

Many thanks to the editors of the following places in which some of these poems first appeared: *Books from Scotland, Denver Quarterly, Five Dials, fourteenpoems, Fruit, Poetry Book Society Bulletin, Poetry Wales, PROTOTYPE 4, Stand, The Good Journal, The North, The PN Review, The Poetry Review, the weird folds: everyday poems from the anthropocene* (Dostoyevsky Wannabe, 2020), *there's nothing here but flesh and bone, there's nothing more* (TULCA, 2021), *100 Queer Poems* (Vintage, 2022) and *Re·creation: An Anthology of Queer Poetry* (Stewed Rhubarb Press, 2022). Some poems also appeared in my pamphlet *Katabasis* (Smith|Doorstop, 2020).

To my students, colleagues, professors, mentors, friends, and family; to Matt and everyone at Carcanet – thank you all for creating this book with me.